how2become

BRNC:
the Complete Guide
to Preparation for
Royal Navy Officer
Training

Shaun McBride

www.How2Become.com

Orders: Please contact How2become Ltd, Suite 14, 50 Churchill Square Business Centre, Kings Hill, Kent ME19 4YU.

You can order through Amazon.co.uk under ISBN: 9781910602423 via the website www.How2Become.com or through Gardners.com.

ISBN: 9781910602423

First published in 2016 by How2become Ltd.

Typeset for How2become Ltd by Anton Pshinka.

Disclaimer

CONTENTS

Part 1

Preparation for BRNC

Chapter 1

Importance of Preparation

'Prior Preparation Prevents a Poor Performance' - Anonymous

If you have been through military selection before, you will be aware that preparation is key. This principle will be just as important throughout your military career. From your interview to your professional training, from driving a ship through a harbour to running a Trafalgar Night ball; preparation will be your best friend. This is a lesson that is especially drilled into Officer Cadets at Britannia Royal Naval College (BRNC). You will prepare for inspections (or Rounds in Naval speak), to lead a boat's crew on exercise, for your Navigation test and finally, for your passing out parade. Those who fail to prepare will fall behind the rest of the class, and often fail altogether. BRNC will push you to your limits, but if you prepare thoroughly, then you can excel.

The reason I have written this book is to allow you to properly prepare. It is my aim to give you the knowledge and tools needed to forge a successful naval career. The fact that you have purchased this book alone shows me that you are serious about preparing for the BRNC – for this I commend you! It is my sincere hope that you will continue to prepare until the day you join the RN, and throughout your career.

Chapter 2

Naval Knowledge & Current Affairs

Why do I need to know about the Royal Navy & Current Affairs?

As an Officer in the Royal Navy, you will be first and foremost a leader. Those that you lead will come to you with questions about all aspects of the Navy, and expect answers. Your credibility as a leader depends on it.

Imagine a newly commissioned officer training aboard a Type 23 Frigate which is expecting a helicopter of the Fleet Air Arm to embark that day. She/he is questioned by a newly trained Seamanship Specialist Able Seaman in his/her division, upon which helicopter is embarking and what its main role is. If the Officer never bothered learning about the Fleet Air Arm, their lack of knowledge will lead them to say that they don't know, or worse, guess and be wrong. The effect of this, compounded with other displays of lack of knowledge, is that the division may begin to doubt their Divisional Officer's credibility and ability to lead. Consequently, the newly commissioned Officer may find it hard to earn their respect or trust, and the essential communications between the Division and the Divisional Officer could break down.

For this reason amongst many, BRNC require a vast knowledge of the workings of the Royal Navy in order to commission. This is, of course, not expected on Day 1, and much of the detail will be picked up along the way. However, the extensive knowledge of the Upper Yardsmen (those who already serve as a Rating and are picked to become officers) and others who know the RN well from the start gives them a huge advantage in all aspects.

With respect to current affairs, it is important to be aware of the world around you. Firstly, staying abreast of current affairs will help your credibility not only with those you lead, but your peers and those who lead you. The higher ranks of Officer all require this awareness, and it will put you in good stead for promotion. As a member of a military service which reacts to events all around the globe, a knowledge of current affairs is essential.

While a knowledge of the democratic elections taking place in Pakistan is not tested or required at BRNC, knowledge of current and recent conflicts such as those in Afghanistan, Iraq, Libya, Syria, and of groups such as Al-Qaeda, Islamic State, Boko Haram etc. will be assumed knowledge. To this end, Strategic Studies are carried out at BRNC, and many current affairs essays will be required in order for you to pass the course.

What do I need to know?

Having passed the Admiralty Interview Board (AIB), you will already have demonstrated a thorough knowledge of the Royal Navy and current affairs. It is important for you to develop this, on a continuous basis, whilst you wait for the chance to join.

Navy Knowledge will take a more practical turn. For example, knowing the exact number of people on a Type 45 Destroyer is not important unless you are on board that ship. However, knowing the capabilities and roles of the ship, how they work with other ships and where they are in the world is much more important.

During BRNC, your knowledge will be developed to a much higher standard, but it is important to start in the right way. In reality, there is no objective benchmark to how much you need to know on Day 1, apart from the Navy knowledge test already done at the AIB. The more you have researched and internalised by the time you start, the better advantage you will have, and the more valuable you will be to your division. The best advice would be to pick up knowledge that is absorbed naturally rather than learning by rote.

Current affairs are, by nature, ever changing. This means that you will need to maintain a constant work rate, in order to avoid falling behind. You will not be officially examined on your knowledge at any time, and again, there is no benchmark to achieve. Strategic Studies lessons are designed to bring you up to a standard acceptable for an Officer on the Trained Strength for military issues. However, life will be a lot easier if you have kept your finger on the pulse.

How do I prepare?

Navy knowledge can be picked up from many different sources. Many of these are interesting in their own right, and should only be used if found interesting. However, they are all excellent for absorbing knowledge without really meaning to:

- **Books** - Historical knowledge can often be picked up from books, many of which are on the 'Reading List' given to you before you join. Other more contemporary books can also give you an insight into life in the RN and broaden your knowledge.

- **Navy News** - A favourite with aspiring Officers. The Navy's newsletter will provide monthly updates on the fleet's whereabouts and activities, and will also include in-depth features that are ideal for passively increasing your knowledge.

- **Personal** - Talking to those already serving in, or have served in, the RN and listening to them *spinning dits* (telling stories) is both entertaining and educational.

- **Visits** - It is far easier to learn about the ship in front of you than the one in a book, and you're unlikely to forget it! Try to organise visits to any naval bases or naval air stations. There is usually a "Visits Officer" of some sort, who you can call or email and see what they can do for you. If you have any friends or family who work on a base, they can "sponsor" and escort you while you look around the base, which is by far the easiest way. There are also a number of organised visits (usually called 'Potential Officer's Courses), about which you should speak with your Armed Forces Careers Liaison Officer (ACLO). Similarly, current affairs sources are better utilised via passive absorption, rather than learning of facts by rote. Many of them will require no explanation.

- **Newspapers/TV Media/Online news sources** - I recommend a variety of sources, from different viewpoints. Using the BBC, the New York Times, Al Jazeera and others will give you a more rounded view of the events going on.

- **Navy News** - As before.

- **Books** - By nature are behind the current affairs, but are good for gaining a more in depth knowledge of a subject, as well as catching up on years' worth of 'news' you may have missed (E.g. The early years of the Iraq conflict due to youth).

Chapter 3

The Kit List

The Official BRNC Kit List

You will receive the full, up-to-date kit list in your joining pack from BRNC. This is only to give you an early idea of what may be required so you can start shopping early.

Required	Recommended	Desirable
Clothing		
Underwear (White bras for females)	Nightwear	
Socks		
Dressing Gown		
Flip Flops		
Civilian Clothes		
Smart Blazer		
Tailored Trousers		
Lounge Suit (Optional)		
Shirts		
Brown or Black shoes		
Tie		
Polo Shirt		
Pullover		
Watch		
Sports wear		
Sports shorts	Tracksuit trousers	
Polo shirt/T-shirt	Sweatshirt	
Trainers		
Swimming Attire		
Sports Bras for females		

General Items		
Permanent markers	Trouser hangers	Dry/Canoe Bags
Clothes name labels	Small/Travel towel	Laptop
Bath towels	Flannel	A4 Notepad
Toilet bag and toiletries	Hands-free attachment for mobile phone	Lighter
Shoe Cleaning Kit	Good Ironing Board	Head Torch (with red filter)
Wooden Coat Hangers	Mobile Phone	Trouser twisties
Small Padlock	Wristwatch with Stopwatch function	Stain Removal kit (e.g. Vanish bar)
Iron	Rules of the Road book	Propelling pencils
Scientific Calculator	Cufflinks	
Pens (Blue/Black)	Nail Brush	
Sewing Kit	Scissors	
	Clothes/Lint brush	

There is no formal muster to check you have all the kit, so there is no need to worry about having everything on here. However, you will be expected to have something on the list if they ask for it. I will now talk about different items on the kit list and why they are needed, and clarify a few terms which may be confusing.

Flip Flops & Dressing Gown

You will be required to wear flip flops and dressing gowns when going to and from the showers, for modesty and hygiene purposes.

Blazer/Lounge Suit

See explanations below for civilian dress. You will be required to arrive in Dog Robbers or a suit.

Sports wear

Sportswear will be only be needed to do your own extra-curricular exercise, and for 'Gash PT' (See below). You will be issued sports kit for your scheduled fitness sessions.

General Items

- Permanent Markers – This will be used mostly to name your issued kit over the first few days. A Sharpie marker is your best bet for this.

- Clothes Name Labels – Iron-on are useful, but often are lost after a few washes. Take spares for this eventuality, or sew a few stiches into the label to prevent it falling off.

- Shoe Cleaning Kit – My best recommendations are "Kiwi Black" shoe polish, a dusting cloth or cotton wool for bulling (shining the toe cap), two brushes (an on/off brush combination for the rest of the shoe) and a spare toothbrush (for the hard to reach places on the shoe). You can look on YouTube for explanations and instructions.

- Wooden Hangers – Take as many as you can. There are limited supplies in the college shop. Plastic hangers were not allowed when I was at BRNC, but that may have changed.

- Good Ironing Board – A good ironing board has a large surface area (width better than length), and has a grippy surface. You will spend a lot of time ironing, so it is worth investing in a good one.

- Rules of the Road book – You are issued with one of these, so I wouldn't recommend spending your money.

- Dry/Canoe Bags – These are for use on exercise to waterproof your kit. It is recommended to get a variety of sizes, from small tablet size to rucksack liner size. The more the better. You may have a chance to buy these or more of these once you've seen your kit and figured out your kit packing plan.

- Trouser 'Twisties' – These are available from the college shop or online. They are to hold the bottom of your trousers over your boots in the correct place (as per uniform requirements you will be shown on your first day).

Civilian Clothes

There are different 'civilian clothes uniforms' that you will be required to adhere to at BRNC. They vary in formality, which reflects their use.

Dog Robbers

The most formal civilian dress at BRNC. This is used as the standard civilian uniform at BRNC, and can be worn anytime you are not in uniform around the college or in the town (except in your accommodation or when exercising). Depending on the decision of the college senior officers, this can be relaxed to Relaxed Dartmouth Rig from Thursday to Sunday. However, this is a privilege rather than a right. It consists of:

- A collared, long sleeve shirt.

- A Windsor knot tie (not clip-on).

- A pair of chinos (The variety of colours found at BRNC is amazing, and bright, unorthodox colours are commonly seen. However, some conservatively coloured chinos are also recommended.)

- A smart black or brown belt.

- A pair of smart, black or brown shoes.

- A smart blazer.

Planters

This is the next most formal dress code at BRNC. It consists of Dog Robbers minus the blazer, and for this reason is usually used instead of Dog Robbers during summer.

Relaxed Dartmouth Rig

This is a smart casual style. It consists of:

- Collared Polo-shirt.
- Chinos.
- Smart, black or brown shoes.
- Smart belt.

Gash PT

This is the least formal of styles. Usually used when no formality is needed, for example, in a rifle cleaning session after an exercise, or when cleaning the accommodation or any number of informal activities etc. It is a flexible 'uniform' which is usually:

- Hoodie.
- Tracksuit Bottoms.
- Trainers.
- T-shirt.

What else should I take?

The following are not included on the official kit list, however, they will make your life easier. These are all recommended by a survey of current and ex-Officer Cadets.

- **A4 Clothes Folder (Search: Flip Fold)** - You will be required to fold to A4 all kit that is not hung up during Rounds. The inspecting officers will be carrying an A4 card to check the size. If you have not tried to 'A4' clothes exactly and uniformly using only an A4 card or by eye, you won't realise how much of a difference this makes. Time is also precious, and this saves a huge amount of time. Highly recommended.

- **Phillip's Azure Iron** - Ironing kit will make up a huge amount of your day at BRNC, especially in the first few days. The need for a quality iron quickly becomes apparent to those who have bought a budget one originally (like myself). The Phillip's Azure cut my average ironing time in 1/3. This iron or another heavyweight quality iron is highly recommended.

- **A Mobile Wi-Fi device** - Besides 3G/4G, this will be your only way of connecting to the Internet in your *cabins* (accommodation) without going to the college library, and is very useful for laptops etc.

Naming of kit

During Rounds (inspections), your items of kit will be checked for naming. This means everything that you own that is on display. Save yourself time at BRNC, and name your kit before leaving. You should do this for everything you pack, as you put it in your suitcase.

Chapter 4

The Reading List

Why do I need to read?

As mentioned, reading is a great way to absorb a lot of the knowledge, tradition and history of the Royal Navy. The reading list has been put together by professors at BRNC, so that you can choose the titles that will be most interesting and educational. All in all, it is designed to give you an insight into the Royal Navy way of life. It will also give you a good start in understanding naval doctrine and procedures. This will help when you must write about such things in your strategic studies lessons.

What do I need to read?

- *Nelson's Way – Leadership Lessons from the Great Commander,* **Stephanie Jones & Jonathon Gosling.**

- *Shackleton's Way – Leadership Lessons from the Great Antarctic Explorer,* **Margot Morrell & Stephanie Capparell.**

- *One Hundred Days, The Memoirs of the Falklands Battle Group Commander,* **Admiral Sandy Woodward.**

- *Gunboat Command,* **Anthony Hitchens.**

- *Armed Action, My War in the Skies with 847NAS,* **Lt Cdr James Newton RN DFC.**

- *One of our submarines,* **Edward Young.**

- *Amphibious Assault,* **Lt Cdr Tristan Lovering RN.**

- *The Royal Naval Division,* **Douglas Jerrold.**

- *The Command of the Ocean, a Naval History of Britain 1649-1815,* **N A M Rodger.**

- *The Royal Navy since 1815, a New Short History,* **Eric Grove.**

- *Seapower, A Guide for the Twenty-First Century,* **Geoffrey Till.**

- *Seapower as Strategy, Navies and National Interests,* **Norman Friedman.**

It is not mandatory to complete this list, and you certainly won't be tested upon it. However, the reading list is a good way to increase your Naval Knowledge and start to absorb the ethos, history and traditions of the RN. The books will give you a rounded strategic view, and the Strategic Studies academic course will be easier for it.

In addition, below I have added some more books that I think would be useful to read before starting BRNC. These are on the whole lighter and more enjoyable.

- **Rick Jolly** - *Jack Speak* - Not a book per se, however it is a large glossary of naval slang which is rich in tradition. It is enjoyable to flick through, and it will help you at BRNC when in dispute with your oppos (colleagues) about the definitions of certain words.

- **Rick Jolly** - *In Confidence* - Another book that's not a book, it is a humorous volume of extracts from annual military reports, showcasing the very finest military humour.

- **Andrew St George** - *The Royal Navy Way of Leadership* - A short book analysing leadership in the Royal Navy. A very interesting read, it will also give context to your leadership lessons.

- **Captain Eric 'Winkle' Brown** – *Wings on my Sleeve* – The story of the WWII Fleet Air Arm pilot who holds the world record for most aircraft types flown. An incredible story.

- **John 'Jack' Moffatt** – *I Sank the Bismarck* – Another great story about the Fleet Air Arm pilot who launched the torpedo that led to the sinking of the Bismarck, the largest German WWII battleship.

Chapter 5

Fitness

Why do I need to be fit?

As a fighting force, every Navy serviceman and woman must be physically and medically fit to carry out their duty in times of war. To be unable to get to a casualty or fire quick enough, or not being able to carry out your duties due to a lack of fitness, is unacceptable and is incredibly dangerous to the ship and its crew. This cannot be relaxed in peacetime. Casualty, fire and other rapid response task forces cannot allow employees more time to get fit enough for war. A continuous level of minimum fitness must be upheld by the entire fleet, in order to allow it to perform to its full potential.

How fit do I need to be?

On joining BRNC, the only real fitness benchmark is to be able to pass the 1.5 Mile Fitness Test, and/or the Multi-stage Fitness Test (Bleep Test) to the correct standard, according to age and gender. You must also be medically fit, which includes staying within the correct weight parameters. This benchmark will exist throughout your entire career, and you will be required to pass it at any time, but at least annually. This is the **minimum** level of fitness expected by the Physical Training Instructors at BRNC.

You will also be required to pass the Swimming Test. This involves treading water for 2 minutes then swimming 50m and climbing out of the pool at the deep end.

If you are unable to achieve these fitness standards you will undertake remedial training in your precious spare time, and if you are still unable to pass, you will be withdrawn from training. It is also frowned upon to fail the fitness test, as it displays a lack of preparation, commitment and self-motivation, all qualities required to be an officer.

TOP TIP: You will usually undertake your first fitness test after 6 days of intense training. You will be unaccustomed to the long days and strain on your body for those 6 days, after which your fitness is tested. For this reason, it is not uncommon to lose time on your normal 1.5 Mile run time. Therefore it is important to prepare for this eventuality by being as fast as possible before joining, to provide yourself with a safety margin.

This being said, a higher level of overall fitness will be expected of you than in the fitness tests alone. Your fitness will improve dramatically in all respects in the time that you are there. However, you don't want to be at the back of the pack and behind the curve. As this is far more subjective, the best advice is to be as fit as possible on arriving at BRNC. You will be less fatigued by the specific *phys* (exercise training) you are given, you will cope better with the very physical challenges of the rest of training, and you will, in general, find the experience less challenging. See below for what types of fitness to prepare for.

What fitness will I be doing?

Period Zero - Twice a week, the college conducts 'Period Zero' sessions before the start of the working day. You will *muster* (meet) outside the college gym at 0600 for a session before breakfast. The session you will undertake will be specific to the requirements of the phase of training you are in. These nearly always take place outside, regardless of weather or season.

The fitness required for this includes a variety of sprints and endurance runs. Therefore you should focus on improving both your ability to sprint and recover, and your jogging. The college grounds sit on a large hill, and this is used for good effect to amplify your training. Getting used to an incline while running will be advantageous. This will also include a lot of body weight exercises: squats, press ups, sit ups etc. Lastly, *leopard crawling* is a favourite military pastime. Search for it on YouTube, and integrate this into your training if you have the inclination.

Initial Military Fitness - Once or twice a week, your division will conduct an 'Initial Military Fitness' class in the college gym hall. This is a package that starts with teaching you how to conduct each section of the session with only a little fitness element, but rapidly ramps up to you completing a session, with fitness based forfeits if you break the rules of the class. The session is similar to 'Drill', where you are given specific orders to complete specific actions, all of which are done in time with the rest of your class. This session not only increases fitness, but instils discipline and loyalty. The session is made up of sprints and jogs, and again, many body weight exercises. The use of equipment for tricep dips, rope climbs and box jumps will also be included.

TOP TIP: IMF Rules to watch out for:

- No moving without being told to, including wiping sweat off your face or itching.

- No speaking.

- Paying attention to the PTI at all times.

- Don't get distracted (and therefore fall out of time with the rest of the class.)

- No moving without a specific order or speaking.

Any of the above will attract punishment by fitness, in an already physically challenging session. This will normally be only for your classmates, while you watch, making you a lot less popular.

Battle Physical Training - Usually at least once per term, you will conduct a Period Zero-like session, competing against another division. This is used to teach the carrying of a stretcher or equipment, as well as to improve fitness.

How do I prepare for this fitness?

Everyone's starting fitness level, preferences and time availability is different, therefore a training plan would be impossible to write, despite its usefulness! With this in mind, devising your own fitness plan is essential. In this section, I will guide you through some of the options that you could include in your plan.

The principle of specificity is important in all fitness. This means if you are training for a marathon, there is little benefit in doing push ups. It is best to train by running. For this reason, use of the previous section for determining what fitness to do is advised. For press ups, practise press ups. For sprints, practise sprints. Working out using resistance machines won't have as much benefit, as the fitness at BRNC will be outdoors and bodyweight focused.

- **Tabata** - a useful way of practising press ups and other exercises is Tabata. This means doing as many press ups as possible in 20 seconds, followed by 10 seconds rest. This is done 8 times, taking only 4 minutes in total. You will be surprised at the difficulty and effectiveness of Tabata!

- **High Intensity Interval Training** - Sprints, followed by short periods of rest (similar to Tabata) are an effective method to improve how long and fast you can sprint, as well as giving you time to recover your breath. Using lamp posts on the street is a popular method of regulating this activity.

- **Cross Fit** - Very popular with members of the Armed Forces, Cross Fit gyms all over the country offer an effective all round fitness training programme. The sessions (minus the Olympic lifting) are similar to the sessions you will find in training.

- **British Military Fitness** - a company that employs ex and serving military personnel, often (ex-)Physical Training Instructors, to run fitness sessions around the country. Again, this is very similar to the sessions you will undergo in training. Therefore, if you are able to get to at least a weekly session, you will be much better accustomed on arrival at BRNC.

Part 2

What to expect at BRNC

Chapter 6

Arriving at BRNC

You've prepared as much as you could. You've packed your kit. You've had leaving parties with your friends. The day has arrived to begin Britannia Royal Naval College, and your career as an officer in the Royal Navy. Congratulations, it's a big day you won't forget.

You will normally be getting a train to Totnes train station in Devon. You may live closer and decide to be driven there. Either way, you will get to Totnes where some already commissioned students will sort you into your new squadrons and divisions, and you'll be hurried onto a bus to take you on the 30-minute drive to BRNC.

Get to know those on your bus. These people will be your life, 24 hours a day for the next 30 weeks. They will be your closest friends, whether you like them or not. Don't worry, first impressions don't stick here. Your impressions of everyone will change hour-by-hour during training.

You'll arrive at the gates to BRNC and as you drive up the hill, you'll get your first view of the college, apart from when you googled it in excitement. You'll file out onto the parade square to be met by Officer Commanding Officer Training, who will welcome you to the college and impart some of their wisdom (this happens a lot at BRNC).

After their talk, you will (attempt to) march off the square (remember always left foot first when stepping off), pick up your kit, and find your new room. You will either be in a 6-8 man room, or in "The Zoo". Along with the slightly smaller "Mini Zoo" it houses half of the intake in two very large rooms.

In your room, you'll find all your new *rig* (uniform), to be fitted, ironed, named and organized over the next few days ready for the start of *rounds* (inspections). Teamwork is crucial for this. Rounds and inspections of kit start within two days of joining so all kit needs to be immaculate very early on.

The Squadron chief petty officer's will show you how to iron clothes, polish your shoes and organize your kit correctly. Then it all starts!

I can only leave you with a few tips:

- On the train, look out for others in suits. Especially the ones carrying far too much kit. An ironing board is a dead giveaway. If you are unsure, conspicuously begin to read a copy of Navy News and if that attracts their attention, you know they're going to BRNC.

- If you do suspect someone on your train to be going to BRNC, make every effort to meet them. One of my best friends was stood on the platform at Plymouth, about 100m down the platform from me, both of us holding ironing boards. We became firm friends on the train. We were then put in the same division, then the same team for our Assessed Basic Leadership Exercise, our Maritime Leadership Exercise and our Initial Fleet Time Oral Board (from an older system of training). A lot of lasting friendships were made on the train to BRNC.

- It is normal to be anxious, but hopefully the remainder of this book will have prepared you for what is to come.

- Despite best attempts, you will probably forget people's names, and everything about them. Don't get too worried about it, everyone is in the same boat *(pun intended).* You will end up asking everyone's name, hometown, and intended branch several times by the end of the first few weeks.

- You will have a lot of kit to fit, name, and then iron. Your quality iron and Flip Fold will help you with this. Get as much done as you can early on, as you will have increasingly less time as your first inspection approaches.

- A major lesson that BRNC drills into you is to help your colleagues. If you have finished preparing your uniform etc. and someone else is struggling, help them to catch up. During Rounds, if someone is obviously behind everyone else, it looks worse on the rest of the room than on that person.

Chapter 7

Your first
two weeks

You will have had a busy first evening in the college, and the pace will not drop off. You are in the 'induction' phase, which is designed to be very busy in order to challenge and improve your time management, organization, team work and your capacity to handle a busy programme. It also is a culture shock: early mornings, late nights, and non-stop work between the two. You will get used to it. Your career won't always be this busy, however, there may be times where the skills you learn here stand you in good stead.

I will now talk about the different activities that you will encounter in the first two weeks. Some will be spoken about in depth in other chapters.

Early Mornings

Generally you will be getting up around 6am in order to get through your ironing backlog (a task that never seems to end for 30 weeks). After breakfast, you will be inspected by your Divisional Officer to ensure your kit standards continue to be high. You will then march off to your first lesson of the day.

Briefs

A lot of your first two weeks will be spent in Caspar John Hall (See 'Places at BRNC' chapter) being spoken to by the different departments of the college, from the Medical Officer, to the lecturing staff. You will be given all the basics that you need to know about life in the Royal Navy, including:

- Ranks.
- Uniforms.
- Rules.
- Security.
- Drink & Drugs policy.
- Basic leadership lessons.

TOP TIP: You will be tired, and being sat in a warm Caspar John Hall will induce sleep. Falling asleep is expected but, of course, very much frowned upon. However, standing up and moving to the side if you are struggling is highly encouraged. Do follow up on this, it's not worth the consequences.

Seamanship

You will visit Sandquay and the Seamanship staff by the waterside. Here, you will begin to learn the required knots and will be shown the River Dart aboard a Picket Boat.

Fitness

You will experience your first Period Zero at 6am on one morning according to the timetable. You will also get your first taste of 'Initial Military Fitness'. On the weekend, you will be required to pass the Fitness Test.

Rounds

Rounds are inspections carried out at 8pm unless otherwise stated, every night for the first two weeks by the College Senior Students or College Staff. The room will need to be clean & tidy, your kit organised and uniform, and you must be in immaculate condition. They will also test your Navy and College knowledge. (See 'Rounds' chapter).

Royal Navy Leadership Academy

This mainly Royal Marine staffed unit will run your leadership development and your end of term leadership exercises (see 'Leadership exercises' chapter). Expect to be taught about *bergens* (rucksacks), webbing, Command, Leadership & Management.

Divisional Exercise

You will explore the area surrounding Dartmouth with your Divisional Officer and your Sea Parents. This is a good chance to get to know them and your division better.

Frantic Friday

Frantic Friday is the culmination of the 'induction phase'. It is a day designed to be the busiest yet, and is your first test as a division. You will be tested on:

- Rules of the Road knowledge.
- Press-Ups and Sit-Ups.
- Teamwork challenges.
- Knots.
- A Stretcher Run (Running a course around the college carrying a stretcher and Dummy).
- Many inspections in different uniforms.

Finally this culminates in Rounds at around 4pm. This is conducted by the Squadron Senior Officer and his team. This will be the hardest Rounds to date. If you pass you will not continue nightly Rounds to the same extent. If you fail, then you must continue the routine until the standards are met.

After Frantic Friday, you will be allowed to go to the Pavilion for your first drink in two weeks, and your first chance to really socialise with your intake.

Chapter 8

Rounds

Rounds are an incredibly important part of life in the Royal Navy. On board a ship, in the middle of the ocean, a fire or flood could be disastrous. With hundreds of compartments on board, it could start from anywhere. Unlike the classic vision of a WWII style army with senior officers in the headquarters and junior officers and soldiers in the firing line, on a ship everyone is literally in the same boat. So, over centuries of history, including three major naval wars fought in the 20th Century, the RN has developed a best practise for reducing the risk of any damage. Part of this solution is 'Rounds'.

Rounds are inspections. On board a ship, this means inspecting almost every compartment, all of which belong to a department or a person on board the ship. They will check for any sources of damage, possible fire hazards, make sure the room is secure for sea (everything is secure, and won't roll around with the movement of the ship) and check for general cleanliness, as even dust is a fire hazard. However, at BRNC, this usually just means *cabins* (accommodation) and *heads* (bathroom).

At BRNC, you will gain a lot of experience of Rounds (as I'm sure you expected already of military life). During your first two weeks, you will conduct Rounds every night, until you pass Frantic Friday's Senior Squadron Officer Rounds. You will then have a different type of Rounds for the remainder of your time in militarisation (more on this later) with the periodic full inspection by various senior staff, like Officer Commanding Officer Training and Commander (Training). Once into Marinisation, you may not have Rounds every night, unless you are on Remedial Training (a punishment). As an officer in the fleet, a higher level of responsibility is bestowed upon you, and you are expected to keep your cabin to the correct standard without it having to be checked every night.

I will now talk about the different types of Rounds and when to expect them. Later, I will talk about what is expected during Rounds:

Open Locker Rounds

This is the most thorough type of Rounds, and will be the type of Rounds conducted until passing Frantic Friday. For the first two weeks, this will be conducted by your Sea Parents, and then increasingly senior staff members: Divisional Chief, Squadron Chief, Divisional Officer and then the

Senior Squadron Officer. Your Sea Parents are College Seniors (recently commissioned but remain at the college for Initial Warfare Officer training) and will be instructed to be incredibly thorough. Should they not have guided you to the right standard by the end of Induction, it also looks bad on them.

Open Locker Rounds include checking everything except one, padlocked drawer (for personal items). This is checking the kit in your wardrobes and drawers, every possible flat surface for dust and everything that can be seen or touched. Later on, I will talk about some of the points they look for.

Closed Locker Rounds

Closed locker rounds will usually be conducted immediately after passing Frantic Friday. These will be conducted by the duty staff members. During this type of Rounds, your lockers and drawers will be shut and off limits, so the staff will mainly be checking the state of the room, which must be to the same standards as Open Locker Rounds.

Duty of Care Rounds

Eventually you will progress to Duty of Care Rounds. You will be informed when Rounds are Duty of Care or Closed Locker through the Squadron notice boards in the New Entry Corridor. Duty of Care Rounds are again conducted by the duty staff members. They are mainly interested in your wellbeing and welfare. The room must be in a tidy condition when the staff members come in, however, they will not search your kit or look hard for dust (obvious surfaces may be felt to make sure you're not completely disregarding cleanliness standards). Be warned however, if your bergen is caked in mud, sat by your bed, they will be inclined and are within their right to look closer and check for cleanliness. This exact circumstance led to us being *rescrubbed* (re-inspected) at 11pm by the PTIs, with a punishing Period Zero session a few days later.

Rescrub

If your cabins and accommodation are not up to the standards, you will be 'rescrubbed'. This means the inspecting officers will return at a time later in the evening to re-inspect the cabin. With Initial Rounds taking place at 8pm already, further rounds will push well into your evening. This is a massive morale killer, and should be avoided at all costs.

What will they be looking for?

Every inspecting officer (Sea Parent or above) is different, and will have their own likes and dislikes. My best advice to you would be to come together and write down every correction or improvement your room received immediately after finishing rounds. This way, you will compile a list of previous pick-ups which you can use to prioritise work and use as a checklist just before Rounds. However, I will give you a list of common pick-ups to get you started. Remember that you are usually in a room of 8, and while it takes hard work to be ready on time, it is very much achievable within the time allowed.

As a previous Sea Parent, this is what I would have expected to find:

- Room to be free of dust, on any upward facing surface within reach. This includes places within reach by standing on desks and by crawling under beds.

- Floor to be clean and vacuumed.

- All kit in drawers is named, ironed and folded to A4, and correctly placed according to instructions you are given. Uniformity between yourself and your roommates is incredibly important. If you have spare No.4 blue shirts in your second drawer, on the left hand side, so must everyone else's shirts be in that same place.

- All kit in wardrobe to be named, ironed, and hung up on hangers (which also must be named and wooden (not plastic)). All buttons on shirts and trousers must be fastened. Kit must be in the correct order (according to uniformity as before) and facing the same direction (again, uniformity). Shoes and boots must be clean and polished, with the laces untied and placed inside the shoe. Caps and Berets to be clean, and correctly placed in the locker.

- Beds to be correctly made. Tucked in on all sides so top sheet is free of creases and is taut. You may need to iron your sheets. On occasion, the pillow may have to be ironed into a Naval Ensign pattern.

- Irons to be emptied of water (some meaner staff may have an imaginative way to remove any remaining water from the iron).

- Ironing boards to be stowed uniformly (usually behind bed frames or in a spare wardrobe).

- Sink to be clean and dry, including the underside of the tap. No drops of water in the sink or on the tap. Use paper towels for this.

- Steel and mirrors to be clean and free of finger marks or smudges, again dry paper towels are useful for this.

- Anything damaged (for example, a cupboard broken before you arrived) must be reported to the Squadron Chief.

- Personal Drawer to be padlocked (or it is fair game).

- Bergens are clean and in a uniform place (e.g. on top of locker).

- Room to smell clean (Air freshener is a good idea!)

- Any additional equipment which doesn't have a specific spot to be stored neatly and uniformly if possible.

- Anything on a notice board must have a pin in each corner (4 pins total).

- If the rope you have been given by the seamanship staff to practise knots on is on display, they may ask you to tie any of the required knots.

- You must be in uniform, correctly dressed and to the correct standard (e.g. No creases, cap to be white).

The standard is high, however, you will be expected to progressively improve. You will not be expected to meet the highest standards on the first night. As with everything at BRNC, staff will usually be happy as long as you have obviously made an effort, are progressing towards the standard, and that you listened to the previous night's feedback and acted upon it. It is unlikely that anyone will be angry the first time telling you, but the second time may attract an angry word or a punishment (like press ups). Feel free to use the above list as a checklist for yourself before Rounds.

In addition to the room, kit and uniform standards, you will be questioned by the Sea Parents and staff about different topics during the inspection. If you do not know something, admit to it rather than guess, and you will have until the next day to find out. As with room standards, if you haven't improved, you may end up attracting punishments.

Next, I will talk about the different topics you may be questioned on, and some example questions (and answers where appropriate).

Naval Knowledge

The staff will look to develop your Naval Knowledge. This includes mostly AIB level stuff and current affairs. I will not need to go into a lot of detail here, as I have spoken about this before. However some example questions are:

- Who is the First Sea Lord?

- Who is the Fleet Commander, other senior naval personalities etc.?

- What is the main weapon system on a Type 23 Frigate?

College General Knowledge

You will be asked a number of questions about college personalities, and about the college in general. There are also biographies of the senior staff around the College, the gist of which you must get to know. It is especially embarrassing when Commander Training asks you who he is, and you are unable to tell him.

- Who is the Captain of BRNC? What was his/her last job?

- Who are other college personalities? What branch are they?

- Who is your Divisional Officer? What is their background?

- Who is your lead Sea Parent? What is their branch?

- Which four names are inscribed on the front of the college? (Answer: Howe, Nelson, Hawke, Drake)

- What is the inscription on the front of the college? (Answer: It is on the Navy, under the providence of God, that our wealth, prosperity & peace depend.)

- What do the chimes of the bell indicate? (Answer: 8 chimes is a new watch (Every four hours). 1 chime means 30 minutes into the watch, 2 means 1 hour into the watch etc.)

- What is the watch system? (Answer: On board a ship you will usually work 1 watch on, 2 watches off. This is how it has worked on RN ships for centuries). For reference, the watches are:

Time	Watch name
Midnight - 0400	Middle
0400 - 0800	Morning
0800-1200	Forenoon
1200-1600	Afternoon
1600-2000	Dogs Watch
2000-Midnight	First

Daily Orders

Daily Orders are placed on notice boards around the college every day. They announce the timings of important events throughout the day, and give information on Sunrise, Sunset, High & Low Tide times & heights, the duty staff members and any important notices.

In order to check that you read and digest Daily Orders every day, you will be questioned on its contents. Some staff may be nicer than others, but assume worst case scenario that they could question you about anything contained on Daily Orders. It's quite a lot to remember, so my advice is to take a photo, and question each other while waiting for the inspecting officer to reach your room.

Rules of the Road

Your Rules of the Road knowledge will be tested on Frantic Friday, and will be developed during Rounds. You may be pushed to learn more if you master this early, but the minimum you need to know is the names of the first 10 rules:

- Application.
- Responsibility.
- General Definitions.
- Application.
- Look Out.
- Safe Speed.
- Risk of Collision.
- Action to avoid collision.
- Narrow Channels.
- Traffic Separation Schemes.

Chapter 9

College Structure

Command Structure at BRNC

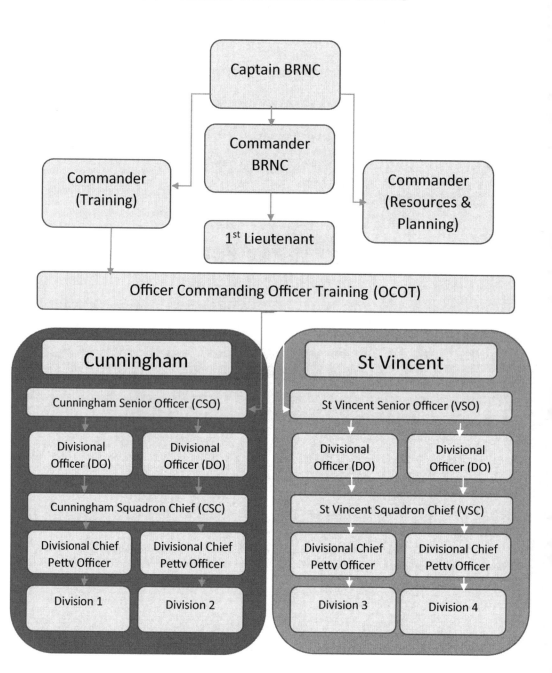

The Command Structure will take some getting used to, but it will become very logical once you've gotten your head around it. It is also similar to the command structure that you'll find on board a ship, base or air station; with some necessary complications.

I will now talk a little bit about the structure, jobs and personalities.

Captain BRNC

Captain BRNC is the College's most senior officer, and is directly in charge of everyone at the College. They are responsible to the Admiralty for the delivery of officers to the Fleet. Similar to a ship's Captain, their word is law.

Commander BRNC

The Commander of BRNC is responsible to the Captain for areas such as discipline, security, staff and College management and day-to-day running of the College.

Commander (Training)

It is the Commander (Training)'s (CdrT) responsibility to the Captain to oversee training, including the efficient running of the training system, changes to the system of training. This person also has the last say in the event of any failures.

Commander (Resources & Planning)

You may not come into direct contact with this Commander as much as the other two, however, Cdr(R&P) is an important force behind the scenes.

1st Lieutenant

The 1st Lieutenant (1L) is a Lieutenant Commander who is responsible for aiding the Commander in his role. The 1st Lieutenant is normally the first call for security, policing and discipline matters.

Officer Commanding Officer Training (OCOT)

OCOT is a Lieutenant Commander who is responsible to Commander (Training) for the effective running of the training system.

Squadrons

The whole College, including staff and students, is split into two squadrons, Cunningham and St Vincent. The two squadrons enjoy a fierce rivalry, and will compete in sports, exercises and more. As a St. Vincent squadron member I am obliged to point out, with an incredibly heavy bias, that St Vincent is the better of the two.

Divisions

All cadets will be split down into divisions of roughly 15-20 cadets. The division will be responsible to the Divisional Chief, otherwise known as Divisional Senior Rate, and to the Divisional Officer. Each intake will normally have 4 divisions, split into 2 per squadron. This means that a squadron is likely to contain 4-6 Officer Cadet Divisions across intakes, and 1-2 College Senior Divisions.

Divisional Officer

Your main point of contact with the staff throughout training will be your Divisional Officer. They will be responsible for the discipline, management, welfare and leadership of your division, and will be close by, for better or for worse, throughout every aspect of your training.

Squadron Chief Petty Officers

The St Vincent Squadron Chief (VSC) and Cunningham Squadron Chief (CSC) are responsible for your accommodation, discipline and day-to-day management throughout training. They will be greatly involved during your induction to the College.

Squadron Senior Officers

The St Vincent Senior Officer (VSO) and Cunningham Senior Officer (CSO) oversee the Divisional Officers of all their squadron's divisions, and are responsible for the effective running, discipline and management of their squadron.

The ranking system doesn't just apply to Officers, but Students too. Below is a breakdown of the Student and Senior rankings.

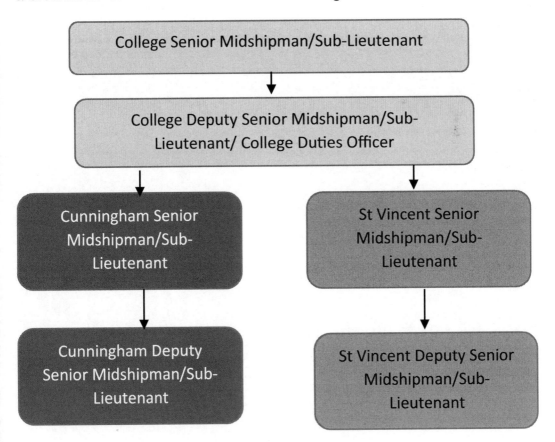

The positions are filled by College Seniors, and are responsible for Student management, including representation of the cadets during meetings, handling of some welfare issues, and the handling of divisional weekly reports.

These will be nominated and chosen by the staff, and will have a number of extra responsibilities and privileges, such as a bigger and better room for the College Senior Midshipman/Sub-Lieutenant.

You will come into contact with the Senior Midshipmen/Sub-Lieutenants during the weekly squadron meetings, and when required will need to write up a report on your week's training, including any problems, so that any concerns or praise can be passed up the chain of command.

Chapter 10

Places at the College

Parade Square

The Parade Square is the large area at the front of the college. This is where drill practise will take place, as well as some fitness sessions, and musters for exercises etc. It is also where Thursday Divisions (a whole college morning parade every week) will take place. Most importantly, it will be the parade square that you conduct your passing out parade on.

The college is elevated from the parade square, accessible by either ramps around the outside, or a flight of steps in the centre. The steps are reserved for commissioned officers and staff, so you will be using the ramps during your time as an Officer Cadet. Similarly, the central 'Front Door' is for commissioned officers and staff, so Officer Cadets use one of two side doors along the front of the college.

Quarterdeck

The Quarterdeck is the central part of the college. Just as they would on board a ship, everyone must come to attention on entering the Quarterdeck. The Quarterdeck is used for many functions, from post-Church tea, to Christmas balls, to a learning environment. It is also a common place to muster for activities.

Junior Gun Room

The Junior Gun Room is where new Officer Cadets eat until they have passed the 'Militarisation phase' and the culmination exercise: 'Assessed Basic Leadership Exercise'. It is located near the 'New Entry Corridor' where you will be living for your first term. All meals will be served in the JGR, as well as morning and afternoon *stand easy* (tea breaks).

Senior Gun Room

The Senior Gun Room is the main eating room in the college. It is located in the front-most buildings of the college. It is for use of Officer Cadets in the 'Marinisation' phase of training. It's a large dining hall, decorated with paintings and RN Battle Honours. It is a very impressive room! All meals will be served in the SGR during your second term at BRNC.

The SGR also has a bar, which is open to senior students in the evenings, and a TV room, and a coffee/tea room.

Wardroom

This is a bar/dining room combination next to the SGR for use of Officers on the staff, visiting officers on courses (such as the Junior Officer Leadership Course) and 'College seniors' (Recently commissioned officers doing the Initial Warfare Officer Foundation Course at BRNC).

College Library/E-centre

This is where your main computer access is. You can access both military (intranet) and civilian (internet) systems. It also has a huge amount of books and resources to help you with your essays and academic studies, as well as extremely helpful staff!

Royal Navy Leadership Academy

Found in 'E-block', the RNLA houses the staff that run your leadership development and also the culmination exercises at the end of each term. There are also more military system computers in 'E-Block'.

Accommodation Blocks

The main accommodation is found in 'D-Block', however there are also overflow rooms in 'C-Block' (to the side of the college) and one or two divisions are usually housed in 'A block' (Front-most building) during the Marinisation phase. 'B-Block' (also in the front-most building) is usually used for staff and visiting officers on course.

D-Block

D-Block is a building that runs parallel to the front-most building, and is mainly accommodation. It has the 'New Entry Corridor' where you will be first housed, including the Zoo and Mini-Zoo. In D-Block is also the JGR and the *NAAFI* (spar shop). In the floors above the New Entry Corridor are where most Marinisation and College Seniors are accommodated.

College Gym

The college gym is a little uphill from D-Block. It contains the gymnasium where you will conduct your Initial Military Fitness sessions and some sports. It also has the swimming pool where you'll be required to conduct the swimming test, and where some fitness sessions are held. The pool is open according to the schedule. There is also a more traditional gym at the back, where you can do your own fitness in your spare time. It is usually open the majority of the day and evening. Alongside it are also squash courts and a bouldering wall.

Sandquay

Sandquay is the college's harbour on the river. This is where you will learn your seamanship skills, including knots, driving a single and twin screw boat, plus yachts. During Initial Warfare Officer Foundation training, you will also be driving larger power boats.

The equipment you'll most commonly use is the motor whalers (single propeller) and picket boats (larger, twin screw propeller). You will be taught to be competent at using both of these, and will be using them during your Marine Leadership Exercise.

The Hindostan

Also found at Sandquay is the Hindostan. An ex-Sandown Class minesweeper, this is now used as a training ship to teach you initial firefighting and flood defence techniques. It is also used as a classroom for seamanship skills, and as headquarters during the Marine Leadership Exercise.

Pavilion

The Pavilion is sat on the Upper Playing Field, and is the bar for officer cadets in their first term. It is open usually only on weekends, and access will be limited depending on your programme.

Lower/Upper playing field

The Lower and Upper playing fields are football/rugby pitches, however, they are also a playground for the Physical Training Instructors (PTIs) during your Period Zero sessions. Here you will also find the Low Ropes and the High Ropes course.

Churches

There are 3 Churches found at BRNC. The main church in the front building is the Church of England church. The Catholic Church is found above the college library, and the Church of Scotland and Free Churches church is found in 'E-Block' with the RNLA. You will be required to attend church (or an equivalent religious ceremony or silent contemplation session for those who wish not to go to attend a religious event) every Sunday that you are in the college (i.e. Not away on weekend leave), and afterwards is a tea/coffee social on the Quarterdeck.

Caspar John Hall

Caspar John Hall (or CJH) is uphill from the Gym. It is a large seating hall where a lot of briefs and mass lessons will be held. You will spend a lot of time in CJH during your first term.

Chapter 11

Jack speak

Jack speak is the word used to describe naval slang. The words have developed and evolved since the days of sailing ships, and a lot of words are rooted in this era. They are still a part of naval tradition, and are especially useful in banter with the other services. The definitive guide to Jack speak is the book of the same name by Commander Rick Jolly, recommended in the Reading List chapter. However, I will give a quick glossary of words that you may come across at BRNC.

- Heads - Toilets/Bathroom. From the age of sailing ships when the toilets were at the front of the ship or "up for'ed".

- Lid - Beret or Cap.

- Wet - Tea or Coffee.

- Cabin – Room.

- Naafi – Tuck shop. From the name 'Navy Army Air Force Institute' that used to run most on base/on board shops.

- Nutty - Sweets, chocolate, crisps, etc. That you can buy from the naafi.

- Goffa - Cans of coke, energy drinks, etc.

- Rounds - Inspections of your cabins.

- Oppo - Colleague.

- Oggin - Water, the sea (Despite arguments to the contrary, you cannot drink 'oggin').

- Muster - To come together or to bring together equipment.

- Dhoby - (pronounced Doh-bee) to wash or clean.

- Flat - a corridor. (e.g. The New Entry flat).

- Pit – Bed.

- Turns & Hitches – Knots.

- Stand easy - A break.

- Scran - Food, or a meal.

- Upper Yardie - Upper Yardsmen, or a rating (usually an Able Seaman or a Leading Hand) who has been selected to become an officer, and will do the full course.

- SUYs - Senior Upper Yardsmen, or a rating (usually a Petty Officer or above) who has been selected to become an officer, but will only do part of the course (due to their wealth of military experience).

- Reggies – Naval policemen/women, from 'Regulators', the old name for the RN Police branch.

- Wren - A female in the RN (from the old Woman's Royal Naval Service or WRNS).

- Matelot - (Pronounced Mat-Low) A sailor, from the French for the same word.

- Crabs - A member of the Royal Air Force.

- Pongo - A member of the Army.

- Bootie - A member of the Royal Marines.

- Dits – Stories.

- To spin dits - To tell stories.

- Throbber - Someone who is too keen.

- Scranbag - Someone who is always scruffy (e.g. you look like a scranbag).

- Rig - Uniform of any sort of clothes.

- Grid – Face.

- Rats – Ugly.

- Divs - Good looking.

- (Billy) Baltic – Cold.

- Tropical – Hot.

- Redders - Very hot.

- Ginners - Lovely weather (Sky is 'gin clear').

- Threaders - Annoyed, agitated.

- Pisswrapped – Wet.

- Hoofing - Brilliant (Very much a Royal Marines slang word).

- Pusser - A member of the Logistics Branch, stores or issued kit (E.g. Pusser's watch vs. A civilian watch).

- Freddie - A member of the Fighter Control branch.

- WAFU - A member of the Fleet Air Arm.

- Stoker - A member of the Marine Engineering branch.

- Jimmy - The First Lieutenant.

- Joss – Head RN Policeman on a ship or base, generally a Master at Arms.

- Divisions - A weekly parade.

- Bulkhead - A wall.

- Run Ashore - A social off-base/off ship.

- Duty Watch Bar - The first bar outside of a Naval base, usually the most frequently used.

- To square away - To sort out.

- Admin - The little necessary jobs like ironing, cleaning, etc.

- Badmin, Admin Vortex, Clusterbomb - Someone who is bad at self admin.

- To beast - To give lots of tough exercise to.

- To get your head down - To sleep.

- Adrift - Absent or Late.

- Rules of the Road - The shorthand name for the International Regulations for Prevention of Collisions at Sea.

Chapter 12

Day by Day,
Week By Week

The aim of this section is to give you a breakdown of your training, week by week, at BRNC. Training at BRNC is very rarely the same for two intakes, as it is constantly being adapted and improved. Therefore no book will be able to give you a concrete explanation of the training. Instead, I will look at some of the common activities you'll conduct and I will provide comment where appropriate on certain days or for the week as a whole. This will give you an idea of what may come. Again, the content of activities is subject to change.

Induction phase:

See the 'your first two weeks' chapter. An intense phase designed to give you basic military skills and to induct you into the military way of life.

NMT100:

You will travel to HMS Raleigh, Torpoint, to learn how to use an SA80 rifle. At the end, you will have the opportunity to fire 25 rounds down the range.

Basic Leadership Development:

You will start on Dartmoor, learning essential field craft skills such as erecting a *bivvy* (a one sheet military tent), how not to be seen, land navigation etc. You will then complete a navigation exercise over Dartmoor, and be taken back to the college. At the college you will complete your first Practical Leadership Tasks (PLTs), of a very similar format to the Assessed Basic Leadership Exercise PLTs. Take note of the feedback, as this may be your last practice before ABLE. You will also spend three of these nights sleeping under a bivvy.

Families' Weekend

Families' Weekend is the first chance you'll have to see your family since starting at BRNC. You will get the chance to show your family around the college (whilst pretending you know where everything is by now) and impress them with all the *dits* you have from training so far. Your family will need to stay in a hotel in Dartmouth or Kingswear. Totnes, Torquay and Paignton are other options, but are a bit further away. Booking early is essential, as the event will usually fill the town's hotels.

You will also get the chance to take your family into the Dartmouth town, usually for an evening meal. Again, booking early is essential to get into the good restaurants.

Assessed Basic Leadership Exercise:

More on ABLE in the 'Leadership Exercises' chapter. Your first assessed Leadership Exercise is in the format of PLTs on Dartmoor.

Royal Marines acquaint:

You will be taken to the Royal Marines Commando Training Centre Lympstone (near Exeter) for briefs from Royal Marines, a tour of Lympstone, and a chance to do the famous 'Endurance course'.

Maritime Leadership Development:

MLD, like BLD, is the preparatory exercise for the Maritime Leadership Exercise. You will conduct more technical and complicated PLTs than during Militarisation. You will do this on the River Dart out of Sandquay, using both Picket Boats and Motor whalers.

Chemical Biological Radiological Nuclear Damage Control week:

This week involves going to HMS Raleigh again in order to learn the basics of First Aid, use of respirators (gas masks) and other CBRNDC measures, including flood defence. You will also get the chance to go in the Damage Repair Instructional Unit (DRIU) that simulates a sinking ship, filling with water through holes that you must correctly repair. (For those who might worry, a mechanism stops water going above roughly shoulder height).

Basic Sea Survival Course:

On this course you will improve your flood defence skills, as well as learning to fight fires. A hugely fun week.

Seamanship weeks:

On seamanship weeks, you will learn to drive a single or twin screw (propeller) boat, including coming alongside and leaving pontoons, man overboard procedures and turns confined space. You will also get the chance to explore the river and learn important rope and knot skills.

Additional Leadership Training:

Following BLD, it may be felt you need another leadership training package in order to prepare you for ABLE, and so you may be recommended for Additional Leadership Training. This is carried out around the college. This is thought of by many as a sign that they have failed BLD, and as a result they become disheartened. However, Additional Leadership Training actually provides you with a great opportunity to complete another PLT, and see several more. You will also have had some time to reflect on your BLD performance and will have this opportunity to try some new improvements. Having done ALTs myself, it was a wholly worthwhile experience, and I was much more confident in my exercises as a result of doing it.

Balls & Dinners

During your time at BRNC, you will experience several balls and dinners. These are formal events that are a proud tradition within the Armed Forces. You will be dressed in uniform and eat in the Senior Gun Room. There are very important traditions to uphold during these events, including passing of port, naval *sea shanties* (naval songs), and a toast to the Queen. The balls & dinners you will likely experience are:

- New Entry Dinner - Roughly Week 5 - This is a training dinner to get you ready for the important ones.

- Burns' Night Dinner – January.

- Easter Ball.

- Summer Ball.

- Trafalgar Night Dinner - November - To celebrate Admiral Nelson's victory at Trafalgar.

- Taranto Night Dinner - November - The Fleet Air Arm's dinner, to celebrate the attack on the port of Taranto during WWII.

- Christmas Ball.

- Passing out Balls.

Passing Out Parade

Your passing out parade will be an important time in your life. You will gain your commission as a Royal Naval Officer and you will have passed the tough BRNC course. You will walk up the central steps for the first time (ish, you have to practise it first) and through the front door of the college. I won't ruin your imagination at this point, I'll let you discover it for yourselves. Of course, your family will all be present to watch too.

Chapter 13

Leadership Exercises

The most important part of BRNC is learning how to become a leader. As an officer, you will be a leader to many people, with a huge amount of influence and power over their career. When individual and group morale is down, they look to their leader for inspiration. However, this is not always a leader in a Napoleon or Nelson style, leading armies and fleets of ships. The 5 sailors on the bridge of the ship need leadership from the Officer of the Watch (driving the ship), and the 15 members of your division from a Divisional Officer. You will also learn how the word 'leadership' is used to encompass two other traits, command and management, also incredibly important to an officer. You may be in charge of Warrant Officers who have served 30 years, and you will need command, leadership and management for this to function properly.

For this reason, Command, Leadership & Management (CLM) is developed and tested in an artificial way through Practical Leadership Tasks (PLTs). You will first encounter PLTs during Basic Leadership Development (BLD) and maybe Additional Leadership Training (ALT). Here your CLM will be developed. Listen well, and take on board everything they say in order to have the best chance to pass the following test: Assessed Basic Leadership Exercise (ABLE).

Assessed Basic Leadership Exercise

The information here is subject to change over time, so use this explanation as a rough guide, not gospel truth. You will conduct Ex. ABLE in week 9 of training, as a culmination of the militarisation phase. It is a 4 night exercise on Dartmoor, Devon. Not only is this a leadership test, this is a determination test. You will conduct PLTs at different places over Dartmoor, requiring you to walk between each. You will be required to carry all your kit with you in your bergen and webbing (a sort of ammunition holder belt), as well as a rifle and all the kit required for PLTs (Wooden staves, ropes). This is by no means unachievable due to the incredible work of the PTIs in your fitness training, even though it may seem well out of reach now. However, a bit of determination and grit is required to combat tiredness and fatigue. If you give in, and pull yourself off the exercise, it will constitute a Voluntary Withdrawal from Training and you will leave the Navy. You may have heard the expression that 'your body can go much further than your mind', however, this was the first time I really learnt this message. (My mind gave up after 30 minutes, my body carried on for 4 days).

You will be required to lead 2 PLTs each as a minimum (some will be asked for a third task). Each PLT will be a scenario in which you must use your equipment and team in a certain way to achieve an objective. You will need to make either a mast or signal flags, cordon off an area or a whole variety of other things. Each PLT will last 30 minutes. You will be assessed on your Planning & Briefing of the task (the ideas you have to complete the task, and how you brief it to your team) and the Execution (the management of the task to complete the objective). If it is not your turn to lead, you will be part of the team helping your *oppo* to pass. You will be expected to *dig out blind* (work hard) for the leader, and you will be assessed on your efforts as a team member, for which you can fail.

During the evenings and nights, lessons and development of field skills will take place, including night navigation exercises, fitness sessions, night raids, camping under a *bivvy*, and wet to dry exercises (getting out of wet kit into dry kit in the correct way). If you are not already soaking wet from the day, they will make sure you are wet at some point. I will leave how they do this to your imagination.

On completing Ex. ABLE, you will decamp and complete a stretcher run to a place where the buses will be waiting for you.

Maritime Leadership Exercise

During the Marinisation phase, you will have completed Maritime Leadership Development (MLD) that runs very much along the same lines as MARL, so you will be comfortable with what to expect. You will be on the River Dart, and you and your crew will have PLT equipment, a motor whaler and a picket boat at your disposal. The exercise lasts for 4 nights.

In a similar format to Ex. ABLE, you will be required to each lead 1 PLT, and some may be asked to complete a second. When not leading, you will make up the team. Due to the more technical nature of the boats, you will also take it in turns to be Executive Officer (Second in Command), Navigating Officer (In charge of navigation for boat safety) and Officer of the Watch (in charge of driving the boat). You will also need two armed sentries on the boat. Again, your effort and performance in each role will be assessed, and this will influence your score. This time, PLTs will last 150 minutes. This gives you more time to plan the more technical tasks that you will be asked to do, and give a longer more complex brief. Again, you will be assessed on Planning & Briefing, and Execution.

During the evenings, designated members will prepare and deliver a brief on the activities and findings of all boats in the task group (the other teams on exercise). Again, staff will be present and you will be assessed. After this, you will conduct a night task, usually on land but sometimes on the river. You will be asked to recover food supplies, extract casualties, capture enemy personnel and run a press conference amongst other things. (These are actually really fun!)

Afterwards, you will be free to sleep, however, two sentries must be on duty at all times (so take it in turns).

On completion of the exercise, you will clean your rifles and boats, and then run with a stretcher and dummy around the college grounds (it is a race).

Passing & Failing

We spoke a little bit about the leadership marking criteria. In every leadership task, you will be assessed on your planning & briefing, and your execution. I will now give examples to illustrate a little bit of what they're looking for in each case, just to give you an idea. You will be given a lot more feedback during your development exercises.

Planning	
Good	**Bad**
Comes up with a common sense plan to achieve the objective. Uses their team (usually second in command) if needed. Listens to ideas of their team, but doesn't have to use them. Plan will use equipment safely.	Is dogmatic in pursuing a bad plan to the detriment of the task and the team. Plan is unsafe. Does not use their team effectively if ideas are needed.

Briefing	
Good	**Bad**
Projects their voice in the correct manner. Articulates plan understandably. Uses the NATO Sequence of Orders. Is delivered from a prominent position.	Does not use the NATO Sequence of Orders. Is quiet and timid. Brief is not understandable to team.

Execution	
Good	**Bad**
Constantly evaluates the progress according to time and effectiveness. If change of plan is required, ensures it is heard and understood. Listens to suggestions of team members. Is in a prominent position to oversee the task. Does not get too involved in the task (unless, for example, 8 are required to lift something, and only 7 excluding the leader, on the team). Motivates and encourages team. Is constantly aware of dangers and limitations and steps in when close to transgression	Does not offer suggestion for change if plan is not working. Does not, or negatively motivates team. Gets too involved in the task to the detriment of management of the whole picture. Limitation or danger transgressed.

You will also be marked on "holistics". This is everything else outside of the above, from being a team member in the task, to how you cope during the walks and night exercises. I will talk about some pointers for this too:

Holistics	
Good	**Bad**
Works hard despite fatigue and tiredness in all tasks. Suggests ideas to the leader during task. Is an optimistic and positive person (even if you are dying on the inside). Is helpful in general.	Takes the lazy option. Hides at the back to avoid being noticed. Constantly complains. Is selfish in general, doesn't help team mates.

Tips and Tricks

As this is an important time at BRNC, I'll leave you with some tips.

- For ABLE, the brief will only need to be quite short, 5-10 minutes total. This leaves 20 minutes to finish the task. You must plan and brief your task according to a set sequence of orders (NATO Sequence of Orders) in that time. Some will think the best idea is to write down everything they are about to say in the brief, heading by heading, during planning, and then read from their notebook during the brief. This will take you at least 15-20 minutes to do, leaving very little time for the task. My best advice would be to write the headings of the NATO Sequence of Orders in your notebook as prompts, but learn to give your mission briefing from memory/a few notes made from when the assessing staff member gave you the information. This dramatically reduces the time needed, as you write next to nothing, and you will have briefed and be working on the task in under 10 minutes. This also avoids the situation when I was on Ex. ABLE, in a 50mph wind, when a friend of mine's notebook page was actually ripped from his notebook by the wind and blew away. This page held his entire brief and he had to do the brief from memory. Notebooks are also liable to get wet (even "waterproof" ones!)

- For MARL however, the longwinded way initially described above is the only option, due to the length and complexity of your briefs. Your briefs may last from 40 minutes - 1 hour in length, and this is impossible to do from memory. For this, prepare a heading by obtaining a crib sheet that you can write in.

- As always, preparation is key. The better prepared you are, the better your score will be, and the more likely you are to pass. If you have your crib sheets etc. prepared by the relevant development exercise, you will be able to get staff feedback on them, and improve them for the real exercise. If the assessed exercise is the first time you use your crib sheets, expect it to have teething problems you haven't ironed out yet, which may reduce your score.

Chapter 14

Tests & Exams

While at BRNC, you will be tested on your knowledge of certain subjects. These will all be progressive, and will all be taught to a more than adequate standard before being tested. This list will give you an idea of some of the skills you will acquire during your 30 weeks at BRNC. The leadership development tests are removed from this chapter as they are discussed elsewhere. The exams listed will have a brief description, but due to development and time, they may change names, times or standard required. However, the rough progression and subjects is what I consider important about this chapter.

- Rules of the Road A - during Frantic Friday. A very basic knowledge of the names of the rules, and a brief idea of what it contains within.

- Rules of the Road B - early Marinisation. A knowledge of how to apply the rules on the water is required, but not a knowledge of every nuance is expected.

- Rules of the Road C - late Marinisation. A knowledge of how to apply the rules on the water, including most nuances, complications and definitions is expected.

- (Rules of the Road during Initial Warfare Officer (Foundation) will be expected to be verbatim knowledge of Rules 1-19).

- Navigation 1 - Militarisation. A knowledge of basic chart principles is required.

- Pre-MARL Navigation exam - Marinisation. A knowledge of how to keep the boat safe on the River Dart is expected.

- Navigation 2 - Marinisation. A knowledge of most chart principles is required.

- Motor Whaler Practical - You must demonstrate the ability to drive, come alongside and leave a pontoon, turn in a confined space and execute a Man Overboard procedure in order to be qualified to drive a Motor Whaler (single screw/propeller). You will also get your civilian RYA Power Boat qualification.

- Picket Boat Practical - Marinisation. Same manoeuvres as a Motor Whaler, but with a twin screw (propeller).

- Turns & Hitches - Frantic Friday. The ability to competently make the required 10 knots.

- Strategic Studies - Militarisation. You will be required to write 1500 word essays on a number of set topics.

- Weapons Handling Test - Militarisation & Marinisation. You will be required to show you can correctly and safely handle an SA80 rifle.

Chapter 15

Leave

Leave is an important part of military life, and also BRNC. It is a chance to get away from the intense training and enjoy getting up late in the mornings and spending all of your hard-earned wages. I will now talk about the different types of leave at BRNC.

College Block Leave

You will be able to take 7 weeks of block leave during the year at BRNC. Block leave means that the whole college is closed and everyone takes leave at the same time. These 3 occasions will be:

- Christmas - Usually from the Friday before Christmas day (circa 20th), to the Monday after New Year's day (circa 5th), 2 weeks leave.

- Easter - Moves with the Easter holiday. Expect sometime in April. 2 weeks long.

- Summer - Usually End of August, 3 weeks long.

Cinderella Leave

Cinderella Leave will be granted towards the end of militarisation or beyond at your Divisional Officer's discretion. It is really only found at BRNC. It is wholly dependent on Divisional Officer, but may be granted for certain (or, if you're lucky, every) evenings and for weekends where weekend leave has not been granted. To be granted Cinderella Leave you must not be on duty at the time. This leave means you are allowed into the town of Dartmouth until **midnight** (hence, Cinderella). You must be pegged back in (There is a peg in-peg out board in the main office) by midnight, when it is checked by the college duty staff member (Officer of the Day). Expect any future leave to be rescinded should you *be* adrift (Late).

Liberty Boats will usually be put in place during your first weeks of Cinderella Leave. At BRNC, they are carried out by the Second Officer of the Day (Duty College Senior) to check that you are correctly dressed to go to the town, and that you correctly peg out before leaving. There are usually two of these, one before dinner (5pm ish) and one after dinner (7pm ish).

Weekend Leave

During Marinisation, weekend leave may be granted, providing you are not on duty over the weekend, but you may get leave for part of the weekend if your duty is on Friday or Sunday, and your DO grants you the permission. You must usually apply in writing using forms found around the college. Weekend leave means you may leave the college after finishing your work on Friday, and must be back by Sunday 23:59 or by Monday 6am (dependent on the regulations according to your phase of training). You must correctly peg out on weekend leave, and place your signed form in a box in the main office. You will usually have to leave the college in Dog Robbers or other civilian dress, but may change into anything once out of BRNC.

Weekend Leave is almost standard within the rest of the fleet, unless you are required to work or are on duty. You will also not need to have written permission once in the fleet.

Chapter 16

College Duties

College Duties will usually begin in the Marinisation phase, however, they are determined by the College Duties Officer (otherwise known as COLDUT) and the staff team, and may take place earlier.

I will list some of the duties to expect. These are not Standing Orders or a checklist, but a brief description.

These are the duties found during Marinisation:

Duty Division

There will be a nominated Duty Division, which will be at hand to respond to fire or other emergencies, as well as to muster when manpower is required. All other duties will be made up by members of the Duty Division.

Quartermaster

The Quartermaster is in charge of the Duty Division and is responsible for ensuring all duties are done. The QM will be required for midnight rounds with the Second Officer of the Day.

Bosun's Mate/Duty First Aider

The Bosun's Mate is required to assist the Bosun (a College Senior) with duties at Sandquay, and will be required for Sandquay Evening Rounds, and for Colours (The raising/lowering of the Naval Ensign).

Ensign Party/Lock/Unlock

Other cadets will make up the Ensign party, and will be required to raise and lower the Naval Ensign at Colours. Usually they will also be responsible for locking up College Buildings at night, and unlocking them in the morning. They may also be responsible for the distribution of Daily Orders (information on the events of the day) and the college mail.

You will come across the following duties performed by College Seniors:

Second Officer of the Day

The 2OOD is responsible to the Officer of the Day (a member of staff) for the running of duties correctly, colours, and conducting of rounds; amongst many other jobs. They are also in charge of the Duty Division. The Second Officer of the Day is incredibly busy, and has usually only just stopped being in the Duty Division themselves, so respect is paramount.

Bosun

This may be the 2OOD or may be a separate duty person. The Bosun is responsible for the safe running of Sandquay, usually during the weekends. The Bosun is also required to conduct rounds of Sandquay to ensure boats are still present and undamaged.

You will also come across:

Officer of the Day

The Officer of the Day is the staff member in charge of duties for the day, and acts on behalf of Captain BRNC. The Officer of the Day will usually conduct evening rounds, and colours.

Chapter 17

Further Information

TRANSPORT

Dartmouth is very cut off from of any major cities or transport links. This was by design of the Admiralty over 150 years ago, deciding being placed in Portsmouth or Plymouth would likely distract the cadets too much.

Car

The A38 between Exeter and Plymouth will take you to Totnes. From there, it is roughly 30 minutes' drive to BRNC. However, the policy is that during BRNC, you are not to drive your car into the college. There is nothing to stop you parking elsewhere nearby, should you wish to take that risk. However, it is advised that you leave your car at home. You are unlikely to use it enough to be worth the hassle. The exception is if you live so far away that it is unfeasible not to have a car for home travel, for example, Scotland, or if there are other extenuating circumstances where you may be allowed to bring a vehicle to BRNC. This is down to your Divisional Officer to decide. During Initial Warfare Officer training after commissioning, you may bring your car into the college.

Taxi

A taxi from the college to Totnes rail station is a normal route to take. This will cost you around £30, however, if you agree to use the same company again, they will often offer you a £5 discount. This is expensive on your own, so sharing the cost is common.

Rail

Totnes Rail station sits on the Penzance to Paddington Line, with some trains to the North of England. Trains are usually every 30 minutes to 1 hour, however, it is important to check as they do vary. Do give the taxi driver your train time when booking, as they are very helpful with getting you there on time.

FAILURE AND BACK-PHASING

'Failure is good. It is a reward for those who succeed.' - Anonymous

Failure is indeed a part of BRNC. You should expect to fail something somewhere along the line, everybody does. However, failing different activities have different consequences.

The tiered warning system

The tiered warning system is in place to give everybody the best opportunity to pass. This structure is used in most naval establishments, with different levels attributed to establishment specific staff. There are 3 levels of warnings:

Tier 1 - Divisional Officer's Warning.

Tier 2 - Senior Squadron Officer's Warning.

Tier 3 - Commander (Training)'s Warning.

Each stage requires an interview with the appropriate person to come up with a plan of action to remedy the failure, after which you may be removed from these warnings. If you are unable to improve after being on a Commander (Training)'s Warning, you will be removed from training.

There are two different types of warnings, one for leadership and other examinations, and one for personal qualities and behaviour.

- If you fail a leadership exercise, you will be moved to a Tier 3 Leadership warning straight away. This means that if you fail another leadership exercise, you will be removed from training. If you failed due to your leadership scores (Planning, Briefing & Execution), then you will be put on the Conqueror training package. If you fail holistically, you will start the phase of training again from Day 1.

- If you misbehave, then the warning will depend on the severity. Subsequent minor actions may move you up the scale.

- If you fail an examination, you will be able to take a re-sit with a little remedial training. If you fail the exam again, you will be put on a Tier 1 Warning. Subsequent failures will move you up the scale.

Compulsory Withdrawal from Training

Should you reach Tier 3 Warnings and still not make the standard, you will undergo a Compulsory Withdrawal from Training, and will leave the Royal Navy.

Voluntary Withdrawal from Training

It should be noted that you can voluntarily leave training at BRNC at any time before passing out. However, you will be removed from the Royal Navy should this happen.

Back-phase

To 'Back-phase' is to join an intake that joined after you did, due to injury or failure.

Conqueror

Should you fail a leadership exercise, then you will be put onto the Conqueror remedial training package. It is a 4 week package of pure leadership development, which works incredibly well. The Conqueror package runs parallel to your new intake's course, and you will join your division a few weeks after they join. A lot of good things are said about the Conqueror package, and many go on to receive top grades in their next leadership exercise.

Protector

The Protector package is for those who have been medically downgraded due to injury. Those in Protector will undergo physiotherapy and treatment, while their division continues to train. Unfortunately, this means that they may be back-phased, but will re-enter training at a point deemed fit by the medical and training staff.

SPORT

Sport is an important part of training at BRNC. Sport develops teamwork, competitive spirit, determination and a number of leadership elements. It is also a good way to wind down, and have some fun during the intense training. It is for these reasons that BRNC recognises the importance of sport.

You will usually, as long as the programme permits, have an opportunity for organised sports on a Monday evening and Wednesday afternoon. All activities are dependent on numbers, but the possibilities include:

- Football
- Rugby
- Squash
- Bouldering
- Gig Rowing
- Clay Pigeon Shooting
- Kayaking

There are also special events organised, to do:

- Surfing
- Rock Climbing
- Orienteering

On top of the normal sports schedule, there will be a possibility to represent BRNC at almost all these sports, and the RN has a society for almost every sport too.

The PTIs will occasionally run an inter-squadron or inter-division sports competition that could include, as well as the above:

- Tug of War
- Sprints

TOP TEN QUICKFIRE PREPARATION TIPS

Before we conclude, I want to leave you with my top 10 preparation tips. These are tried and tested pieces of advice, which I myself used to get through the training.

1. **Get fit** - Get as fit as possible, this will remove a huge source of stress and time at BRNC.

2. **Improve your essay skills** - If essay skills are a weakness, practise. You will be required to write many 1500-2500 word essays in your time at BRNC.

3. **Be proactive** - Start as early as possible so that you can fit in more, and you won't be under as much pressure in the days leading up to joining.

4. **Manage your time** - Time invested before BRNC under no pressure will save you time, especially when you are under immense physical and time constraints.

5. **Have the right attitude** - The military expects a can-do, optimistic attitude. Remain this way throughout your preparation.

6. **Have realistic expectations** – In training, the Navy will never expect you to know something you haven't been taught, be capable of something you haven't been shown or to do something you haven't been told to do. This fact should allay your concerns about needing to be 'good enough' before BRNC. Preparation will make everything much easier, but is not mandatory (There are stories of cadets who are given just 24 hours' notice before arriving at BRNC).

7. **Be positive** - If you already have a place, it is because the Admiralty Interview Board saw your spark of potential, which will be developed at BRNC.

8. **Connect with others** - Try to find other people who are joining BRNC at the same time as you (maybe through the 1 day course offered by How2Become!) – Or you can set up a Facebook group which others may find!

9. **Plan ahead** - Try to finish old projects and personal admin before BRNC as you will have little time to manage your outside life, especially in the first 10 weeks.

10. **Prior Preparation Prevents a Poor Performance.**

A Few
Final Words

I would like to finish by congratulating you on getting this far on the way to being a Naval Officer, and by wishing you luck on the next stage of your adventure. Your time at BRNC will be filled with extreme highs and extreme lows, but you will always look back on it as a hugely fun and rewarding experience. It will provide you with the important skills, such as discipline, determination, time-keeping and organisation, which will stay with you for life. Whether you decide to stay in the Royal Navy until aged 55, or leave after just a few months, it will be a life changing and positive experience.

If you are looking for more information, I would strongly advise that you attend the weekend course related to this book. On this course, you will receive much more information on practical training and more details than I couldn't fit into these pages. This includes:

- Fitness.
- Knots.
- Rounds & Personal Administration.
- Uniforms of the Royal Navy.
- Leadership exercises.

As well as this, you will meet others going to Britannia Royal Naval College before the big day itself, and receive detailed explanations on any questions you might still have.

For more information, visit the **How2Become.com** website.

If you have found this book useful, especially if you have just commissioned, or if you have any comments, please get in touch by emailing **shaun.mcbride@ hotmail.co.uk** and let me know whether I have made a difference! Thank you.